Living Through History

BRITAIN IN THE 1950s

PAT HODGSON

B.T. Batsford Ltd London

CONTENTS

Typeset by Tek-Art Ltd, West Wickham, Kent
Printed and bound in Great Britain by
Courier International Ltd, Tiptree, Essex
for the publishers
B.T. Batsford Ltd
4 Fitzhardinge Street
London W1H 0AH

ISBN 0 7134 5838 0

ACKNOWLEDGMENTS

The Author and Publishers would like to thank the following for permission to reproduce illustrations: W.H. Allen for figure 32; BBC Hulton Picture Library for figures 9, 11, 12, 14, 15, 18, 19, 20, 21, 22, 23, 28, 29, 30, 31, 33, 36, 38, 39, 41, 43, 48, 50 and frontispiece; A. Bell & Co for figure 5; Bodley Head/University of Reading for figure 35; Bowater Industries for figure 7; British Airways for figure 46; British Telecom for figure 47; Camera Press for figure 44; Design Council for figures 4 and 45; Esso for figure 6; The Ford Motor Company for figure 49; Pat Hodgson Library for figures 27, 40 and 53; Pat Hodgson/Raymond for figure 52; Pat Hodgson/Singer for figure 2; Pat Hodgson/George Thomson for figure 26; Jacqumar for figure 51; Imperial War Museum for figure 17; Osbert Lancaster/John Murray for figures 13 and 24; Popperfoto figure 34; Pye Ltd for figure 37; Sainsbury PLC for figure 1; Tommy Steele 42; Leslie Thomas for figure 25; Three Castles for figure 10; Victoria and Albert Museum Press Office for figure 54; The Wedgwood Museum for figures 3 and 8. The pictures were researched by Pat Hodgson.

Frontispiece
Tommy Steele pictured early in his career.

Cover pictures
The colour photograph shows Tommy Steele with some young friends in 1956. The bottom left illustration shows the cover to a Festival of Britain programme (1951), the bottom right illustration shows a Butlins Holidays advertisement (all pictures courtesy Pat Hodgson Library).

AN END TO AUSTERITY

The fifties have been overshadowed by the war which preceded them and the lively sixties which followed. Although fifties fashion and music are having a revival today, it is still difficult to understand what it was like to live at that time. History rarely falls neatly into decades and the fifties are no exception. In the first few years Britain was still recovering from the war, but by 1959 Harold Macmillan was able to boast, 'You've never had it so good', and an artistic and social revolt against the Establishment had started which continued into the sixties.

If a time-traveller from the present day could be taken to a British town in 1950, he would immediately notice the dilapidated, unpainted buildings and the shabbily-dressed people. Although five years had gone by since the end of the War, there were still gaps between buildings caused by bomb damage. Few cars were on the roads and people used bicycles or public transport.

Labour had been in power since 1945 and laid the foundations of the welfare state, but had also faced post-war balance of payment problems. As a result, the best British goods went for export and little was imported from abroad. Even patterned china was not available for the home market and Britons had to be content with white or pastel shades. Many kinds of food, such as butter, bacon, meat, tea and sugar, were still rationed and

1 Sainsbury's Blackfriars branch in 1952, when meat was still on the ration. Only large families had enough 'points' to purchase a small joint and people generally ate meat once a week.

Cinders & Buttons & Beaus

' Poor Cinders ! The date of my dreams and the same old dress, but *Fairy Godmother*, the Singer Shop, waved the magic wand . . . Lo and behold . . . a helpful assistant, oceans of sewing notions,

and my own material made up the Singer button, buckle and belt service . . . everything for my transformation scene. It was all *sew easy!* " What a stunning dress," said Prince Charming.'

Every sewing notion and service at one shop – if one shops at the SINGER shop

SINGER SEWING MACHINE COMPANY LIMITED, SINGER BUILDING, CITY ROAD, LONDON, E.C.1

2 Singer Sewing Machine advertisement in 1950. Most people still found it best to make their own clothes, as cheap, fashionable garments in man-made fibres were not plentiful in the shops until the late fifties.

would remain so until 1954. Few people ate in restaurants as the five-shilling limit on meals was not removed until May 1950. Recipes of the period recommended the use of dried egg and suggested making 'Mock Cream' with a mixture of milk, cornflour, margarine and sugar, as the real thing was unobtainable.

A 'points' rationing system for clothes had been abolished in 1949, but there was still little choice for women. Nylon stockings were scarce, although sometimes 'export rejects' could be found in shops or from a 'spiv' on the black market. Men wore drab 'Demob' clothes – generally a sports jacket and baggy trousers or an ill-fitting suit – given to them in exchange for their uniform when they left the Army.

Looking back on the early fifties, Neal Ascherson described them as 'the years on the grey plateau . . . everything dangerous or vivid lay in the past' (*The Observer*, June 1987). On an average wage of £6 8s a week there was little to spare for entertainment. Suburban High Streets were deserted at night. An evening out for young people generally meant the pictures or a dance. Couples were often chaste as they had nowhere to go to be alone together. In the pre-Pill age birth control was unreliable, abortion dangerous and illegitimacy frowned upon. Girls married early and settled down to family life like their mothers. Although Labour had started to tackle the shortage of housing, much had yet to be done. Many lived in 'prefabs' – prefabricated houses which had originally been put up as temporary accommodation, but were to remain part of the urban scene for many years to come.

Towns were much dirtier than they are today, in spite of the lack of cars on the road. Before the Clean Air Act of 1956 smoke from factory chimneys and coal fires polluted the atmosphere causing 'smog' – a combination of smoke, fumes and fog – which made clothes

3 Mug made by Wedgwood to commemorate the Festival of Britain in 1951. The Festival logo is on the front.

and homes filthy, often causing the deaths of old people or those suffering from lung diseases.

The Festival of Britain brought new life into this grey world in 1951. Labour Minister Herbert Morrison had first planned the event in 1947, but by the time the Festival opened there was a Conservative government, which was to remain in power for the rest of the period. London was transformed by the Festival. In *A Tonic to the Nation* John Mackay remembers how impressed he was with the Dome of Discovery, feeling the 'newness of everything' and a 'sense of pride' in his country's future. In the same book Gwendoline Williams recalls the Festival Gardens and funfair at Battersea: 'It was fun to cross Chelsea Bridge and enter the enchanted world of the gardens . . .'. The Battersea Funfair, the Festival Hall and National Film Theatre remained as permanent reminders after the Festival was over.

Apart from giving the British new hope in their future, the Festival promoted a style in architecture and design known as 'Contemporary', which rapidly spread across the country, influencing a generation. Describing a 'Contemporary' living room,

A.S. Byatt writes: 'The walls, in a way that was fashionable in those post-festival years, were all painted in different pastel colours: duck-egg blue, watered grass-green, muted salmon rose, pale and sandy gold. The armchairs were pale beach, upholstered in olive cord.' (*The Virgin in the Garden*.) People painted their houses and put out window boxes, restaurants opened and towns became more cheerful places. The Coronation of Queen Elizabeth II in 1953 was another cause for celebration, some seeing it as the dawn of a New Elizabethan age.

The Festival was also a stimulus to the arts. Sixty painters and 12 sculptors were commissioned to provide works for exhibition, among them the painters John Piper, Lucien Freud, John Minton, Ben Nicholson and Graham Sutherland, and sculptors Henry Moore, Jacob Epstein, Reg Butler and Barbara Hepworth. Coventry Cathedral, designed by Basil Spence and commissioned in 1951, was a lasting monument to Festival style. The Council of Industrial Design (now

4 Room setting in the Homes and Gardens Pavilion at the Festival of Britain, 1951, showing the 'Contemporary' style of furnishing.

The Design Council), which had played an important part in the Festival, became a powerful arbiter of taste in the fifties and sixties.

The deterioration of relations between East and West cast a shadow over the decade and nuclear war became a terrible possibility. In 1956 the brutal suppression of the Hungarian Revolution by Russia showed the cold face of Communism to the world. Young men still had to do compulsory National Service and many saw active service in Korea, the Canal Zone, Cyprus, with the British Army of the Rhine, and in other parts of the world. The fifties also saw a loosening of Commonwealth ties, and the gradual realization that Britain was no longer one of the leading powers, but that her future lay with America and Europe.

Scientists were horrified by the proliferation of nuclear weapons. In 1955, 52 Nobel Prize winners signed an appeal warning the world that 'whole nations, neutral or belligerent' could be wiped out, stimulating a lobby for nuclear disarmament. Britain's first nuclear power station, Calder Hall, was opened 1956 and hailed as the first plant to harness atomic power for peaceful purposes. No one knew at the time that it would also be producing plutonium for military use. When a fire broke out at the Windscale nuclear plant in 1957, the British public were not told that it caused a radioactive cloud to drift over most of England.

A journalist called Henry Fairlie coined the word 'Establishment' in the early fifties to describe those with the power in Britain, who appeared to have a stranglehold on politics, art and social attitudes, mainly because they had been to the same schools and universities. Returning ex-servicemen, many of whom had university grants, were unwilling to return to the pre-war *status quo*.

1956 is now considered to be the turning point when the old guard lost ground, partly because it was the year of the Suez Crisis, when Britain discovered that she was not powerful enough to pursue an independent, imperialist policy in the face of United States opposition. The same year also saw the beginning of an anti-Establishment move-ment in literature and the theatre by those who became known as 'Angry Young Men'. The Establishment had received an earlier blow when the spies Burgess and Maclean defected to Moscow in 1951 and it became clear that they had not been suspected sooner because they came from the same social class as their seniors at the Foreign Office.

In 1956 teenagers began to be a social force to be reckoned with. As there was little unemployment, many young people now had lucrative jobs with money to spend on clothes

5 Advertisement for a slow-burning fire, 1952. Most households still had open fires in the early fifties, which had to be laid, lit and cleared-out daily. The slow-burning fire was easier to maintain and used coke and lower grades of coal, which was useful at a time of coal shortages. Housewives in fifties advertisements were generally shown wearing frilly aprons and doing the chores.

You light this fire... only ONCE A WEEK

Get a GLOW or a BLAZE

Controlled draught.
5-7 day Ash-can. No unsightly attachments.
Reduces room draughts.
at a touch of the lever !

It's true—the B SUPAHEAT FIRE ne lighting only once a we and burns any kind of f Coal of all grades, co etc. This modern ope hearth fire will b slowly all night long a will burst into a chee blaze whenever you ne it. *Write for full deta*

BELL SUPAHEAT **Fir**

and entertainment. Rock 'n' roll music came over from America and Tommy Steele became Britain's first home-grown pop star. A new teenage culture sprang up with its own music, meeting places and clothes, common phenomena today but quite new in the fifties. Gangs of 'Teddy Boys' were often feared when they carried their anti-social behaviour to extremes, and some helped to provoke race riots at Notting Hill Gate in 1958. The number of immigrants from the commonwealth, particularly from the West Indies, increased in the fifties and many encountered racial prejudice in their homes and workplaces, as well as from street gangs.

Reacting against the War, women during the fifties decided to become housewives again, after doing men's jobs in the forces and factories in wartime. Few married women now worked and equal pay was virtually non-existent until granted by the Civil Service in 1958. In 1954 the average annual wage for a man was £546 13s and for a woman £276 10s 6d. *The Guardian* reported in 1959 that a group of Girton graduates had agreed that politics was not a good career for women and 'only the exceptional woman is now going to go on working outside her home' after marriage. Advertisements were blatantly sexist, emphasizing women's domestic duties – something which television helped to promote when commercial television was introduced in 1954. *Picture Post* worked out in 1954 that a woman spent at least five hours in the kitchen each day. Even the elaborately corsetted fashions of Dior, Sarah Mower of *The Guardian* realized with hindsight, 'encapsulated the spirit of the good little wife, the ideal woman of the fifties' (26 March 1987). The status of women in the fifties led to the women's liberation movement of the sixties.

6 Children at school in Fawley. When the giant Esso oil refinery was opened there in 1951, the increase in population caused acute overcrowding in local schools and Esso provided extra accommodation for the children. By the end of the decade the refinery was a major source of petrol for private cars and industry.

THE NEW ELIZABETHANS

The monarchy helped to revive a sense of pride in being British during the fifties and kept the Commonwealth united in times of change. George VI was deeply mourned when he died in 1952, but the Coronation of a new Queen symbolized a new beginning and comparisons were made between the young Queen Elizabeth and her Tudor predecessor – who had been the same age when she was crowned. The press christened her subjects the 'New Elizabethans', *Picture Post* proclaiming 'A New Reign and a New Challenge' (19 April 1952). There were celebrations throughout Coronation year all over the country. On Coronation day (2 June 1953), thousands of people lined the route in spite of wet weather. Ivor Brown, writing in *Country Life* (June 1953), commented 'Those myriads who had sat all night on the pavements contained an astonishing number of grey heads. The people of London were well schooled in 1940 to doss anywhere.' When it was announced to the crowd that Edmund Hillary had climbed Everest there was an exciting feeling that that everything was possible in the new reign.

It was the first time a Coronation had been televised and people asked their neighbours in to watch, as few had sets. Transmission was in black and white and the chief commentator was Richard Dimbleby. His sense of occasion and reverence for the monarchy helped to make the broadcasts memorable and to establish the myth of a New Elizabethan Age. Newspapers were filled with articles and photographs about every aspect of the Coronation. The *Daily Express* compared typical New Elizabethans Edmund Hillary, Henry Moore, Benjamin Britten and Frank Whittle with their Tudor predecessors Shakespeare, Drake, Raleigh and Marlowe. *Picture Post* made another list, which included Earl Mountbatten, Graham Greene, Sir Hugh Casson, Sir William Walton, Graham Sutherland, Stirling Moss, Margot Fonteyn and Alec Guinness.

There was an inexhaustible interest in the

7 The coronation in 1953 was celebrated all over Britain. This typical village party is taken from an advertisement of the time. A Boy Scout helps to serve the tea.

8 Tea set made by Wedgwood to commemorate the Coronation. By 1953 coloured china was available again for the home market.

Queen and Royal Family throughout the period and Royal tours to various parts of the Commonwealth were covered in detail by press and television. There was great interest in the royal children – at the time of the Coronation Prince Charles was four and his sister Anne not yet three. However, a book of reminiscences by ex-Royal governess Marion Crawford ('Crawfie') was not well received.

The Queen's sister Princess Margaret also attracted a good deal of press attention as she was in her early twenties and there were hopes of another Royal wedding. Unfortunately, Group Captain Peter Townsend, with whom she fell in love, had been divorced and royal advisors felt that this marriage might undermine the Queen's position as Head of the Church of England. In 1955 the Princess issued a statement saying that 'mindful of the Church's teaching that Christian marriage is indissoluble, and conscious of my duty to the Commonwealth', marriage with the Group Captain would not take place.

Towards the end of the fifties a more critical attitude to the monarchy and to the Establishment generally developed. Lord Altrincham complained about the Queen's 'woefully inadequate training', describing her style of speech as 'frankly a pain in the neck' and likening her words to those of 'a priggish schoolgirl, captain of the hockey team. . .' (*The National and English Review 1957*). Soon afterwards Malcolm Muggeridge asked in the *Saturday Evening Post*, 'Does England Really Need a Queen?'. Although the majority of people still supported the Queen and the Royal Family, anti-royalist feelings caused her advisors concern.

Richard Dimbleby (1913-65)

The Coronation marked the beginning of the television age. 'It wasn't till after the Coronation that you suddenly heard people saying, "Did you see such and such on TV?".

Before then it had never been a topic of conversation', remembers Maggie Saunders, an Assistant Floor Manager (*Coming to you Live*). As a television personality, Richard

9 Richard Dimbleby and Anona Winn take part in the Radio Show *Twenty Questions.*

Dimbleby was instrumental in creating a reverence for the monarchy and interpreted the Queen's position in the modern world. Dimbleby had joined the BBC as a reporter in 1936 and became well-known as a war correspondent. From the beginning of his career he saw the importance of on-the-spot reporting and often disagreed with the BBC hierarchy. His historical war-time broadcasts included a mission with an RAF bombing raid on Berlin in 1943, coverage of the D-Day landings in Normandy, a report made as first correspondent at the liberation of Belsen and a description of the Allied entry into Berlin.

In spite of his distinguished career, the BBC had little to offer him in 1945 and he resigned in order to become a freelance. He was soon working on two radio programmes for his old employers – *Twenty Questions* and *Down Your*

Way, the latter enabling him to develop his technique of conducting an unscripted, unrehearsed interview. When television started up again after the war Dimbleby realized its importance and managed to become one of the commentators for the Victory Parade in 1946. In 1949 he was an interviewer on a new television programmed called *London Town*, which was succeeded by *This Land of Ours* in 1952. By the time of the Coronation he had become the best-known television and radio commentator and was the obvious choice to report the ceremony for the first time on television.

The BBC under Lord Reith had always promoted a deep reverence for the Crown and reported all royal events. Richard Dimbleby also had an instinctive respect for royalty and understood the importance of the monarchy in safeguarding the British way of life. His report of the funeral of Queen Mary (for television), the lying-in-state of George VI (for radio) and

At Picnics today
the New Elizabethans
crown their enjoyment
with

The
"THREE CASTLES"
Cigarettes

20 for 3/11d.

---

10 Coronation year advertisement for Three Castles Cigarettes, using the phrase 'New Elizabethans'. Most people smoked in the fifties and research had not yet shown that cigarette smoking was linked with lung cancer.

the funeral of the King (for television) had given him experience of royal occasions. He wanted viewers to understand the 'deep religious significance' of the Coronation. 'I was deeply conscious not only of the responsibility upon my own shoulders, but of the tremendous duty that rests upon the television service as a whole . . . it is a mirror held up to the life of the nation.'

There had been some doubts about whether the Coronation would be televised at all as Churchill and his advisors were against it. When agreement was finally reached, there were strict regulations about photography in the Abbey. Peter Dimmock, the BBC producer of the programme, remembers being told that cameras should not come nearer to the Queen than 30ft. 'What they didn't know, and what I knew', he says 'was that on the day I'd use a 12-inch lens and I'd get the Queen in close-up' (*Coming to you Live*).

Dimmock also remembers how quickly Dimbleby adjusted to unforeseen events. During the Coronation ceremony Princess Margaret's procession arrived early, while Dimbleby was naming the ambassadors. 'The ambassador we had the camera on happened to stand up just as I screamed into Richard's headphones, "Richard, Princess Margaret's procession's coming under the choir screen!". And without a moment's pause, Richard said, "And now he stands, as well he might, to greet Princess Margaret's procession" – so allowing me to pan the camera straight over. He was so quick, so adroit – a dream to work with.'

After the Coronation the general public associated Dimbleby with state occasions and in later years he was continuously asked for his views on royalty. His news reporting was also renowned and he took part in several memorable programmes for the BBC, among them the current events programme *Panorama*, which started in 1953. When he was anchor-man for the first General Election results special, Peter Black wrote in the *Daily Mail*, – 'From all the hours that I was watching I recall only one unrehearsed incident; the extremely gratifying sight of Richard Dimbleby eating a biscuit. I congratulate Dimbleby on the most impressive performance of his career. . . .'.

In 1957 Dimbleby introduced the famous spoof film for *Panorama* on the Swiss Spaghetti Harvest. The film was shot in Switzerland, where spaghetti was hung from trees and Dimbleby solemnly commented 'this marvellous festival. The first harvest of

11 Richard Dimbleby taking part in a television series *About Britain* in 1953. He is photographed making a trip to the Goodwin Sands in the Walmer Lifeboat.

the spaghetti.' The cameraman recalled how 'At the end of the three-minute film Richard Dimbleby said, "Now we say goodnight on this first day of April", but so great was the public's trust in their commentator, that most viewers were taken in.

Dimbleby remained a freelance, but loyal to the BBC, who often attempted to get him back on the staff, as they were afraid of losing him to Independent Television. Between 1950 and the time of his death in 1965 he covered over 500 outside broadcasts for radio and television and 150 important state occasions, many of them royal.

In spite of his devotion to the Royal Family, Dimbleby did not move in Royal circles and was hurt that the Queen never included him in her informal gatherings to meet her subjects.

He was used to cricism, within and outside the BBC, but adverse remarks increased in the late fifties when people were beginning to question the Establishment. Cassandra of the *Daily Mirror* described him in 1956 as 'the royal radio Pussy Cat. . . To listen to Mr Dimbleby describing a royal occasion is like tuning in to an oily burial service.' A new style of interviewer, typified by Robin Day, was becoming popular. But in spite of ill-health Dimbleby still commented on the big occasions – Princess Margaret's wedding (1960), the first BBC transmission from Moscow (1961), the earthquake disaster in Skopje (1962), President Kennedy's funeral (1963) and the funeral of Sir Winston Churchill (1965) among them. When he died Huw Wheldon, Controller of Television Programmes, said, '. . . he was the voice of our generation, and probably the most telling voice on BBC radio or television . . . I feel he is irreplaceable. . .'.

Cecil Beaton (1904-80)

'Cecil Beaton is one of the latest in a long line of royal iconographers which stretches back to the Norman Conquest of England' (Peter Quennell, *Royal Portraits*, 1963).

If Richard Dimbleby was the publicist of the New Elizabethan Age on television, Cecil Beaton was its image-maker. He was a devoted monarchist, photographing the Royal Family during the fifties and sixties – and his diaries describe Establishment figures of the day. His theatrical designs were some of the most brilliant in the established theatre of the fifties.

Cecil Beaton came from a middle-class background and was educated at Harrow and Cambridge, where he first became interested in photography, design and the theatre. Beaton left university without a degree but

with influential friends. In London he soon found portrait photography brought him into contact with society life. Early on in his career, he wrote in his diary:

Photographs are a good excuse to see people and luckily the day has not yet come when beckoned people do not come (November 1936).

By 1939 Beaton had made a name for himself in photography, theatre and fashion. He had

12 Judges at the English Opera group's costume ball at the Festival Hall in November 1952. Cecil Beaton is second from the right. 'New Elizabethans' Moira Shearer (ballet dancer) and John Mills (film star) are on the left of the group. The Festival Hall opened in 1951 for the Festival of Britain.

He had also received his first commissions to photograph the Royal Family. After taking photographs for the Ministry of Information during the war, he resumed his old life in London. He was given more royal assignments – in 1948 he photographed Princess Elizabeth with her first baby, Charles – but was worried that he would not be asked to take the official portraits for the Coronation. The photographer Baron was now a formidable rival as he was a friend of Prince Philip's. It was with 'enormous relief' that Beaton received 'the call saying the Queen wanted me to do her personal Coronation photographs' (*Diary*, May 1953).

Watching the ceremony from his seat in the Abbey, Beaton observed the Queen:

Her cheeks are sugar pink, her hair tightly curled... As she walks she allows her heavy skirt to swing backwards and forwards in a beautiful rhythmic effect.

After the ceremony he took the official photographs at the Palace. He photographed the Queen against a blown-up photograph of the Abbey – she confessed, 'the Crown does get rather heavy'.

Beaton's career as royal photographer continued into the 1970s. In 1955, when he photographed the Queen before she left on a Royal Tour of Nigeria, he wrote:

Luckily it seems that the Royal Family have only to get a glimpse of me for them to be convulsed with giggles. Long may that amusement continue for it helps enormously to keep the activities alive.

The Queen was not made-up professionally before being photographed at this time, which made Beaton's job more difficult.

In the late fifties Beaton feared that Anthony Armstrong Jones might supersede him as royal photographer, and this became a real possibility when Armstrong Jones married Princess Margaret in 1960. However he was again made official photographer at the wedding. His diary comment on the bridegroom was that he

looked extremely nondescript, biscuit-complexioned, ratty and untidy . . . 'he is in no way romantic (even as Townsend was)' but 'he is the man the Princess has fallen in love with . . .' (May 1960).

More royal commissions followed. Beaton always found the Queen Mother very sympathetic but wrote of the Duke of Edinburgh: 'The opposition of "this hearty naval type" must be contended with . . .'.

Sir Roy Strong believed that Beaton's photography created

a new mythology of monarchy. . . Before that the Yorks had no image. . . He had the most incredible eye. He always cared about the monarchy with tremendous passion. (Quoted in Hugo Vickers' *Cecil Beaton*.)

Among the many books Beaton published was a collection of Royal Portraits in 1963. He sent a copy to the Queen Mother, who replied, 'I find it very nostalgic looking through the pages. . . I feel that, as a family, we must be deeply grateful to you for producing us, as really quite nice and *real* people.' (*Diary*, May 1962.)

Cecil Beaton was dazzled by the narrow society world which was still dominated by the pre-war class structure in the early fifties. The press reported the escapades of aristocratic families in the way that they later followed pop stars and sports personalities. In 1954 Nancy Mitford coined the expression 'U' and 'Non-U', describing the habits which distinguished the upper classes from the rest – something which started as a joke, but had an element of truth. It was not until the sixties that the leaders in society changed radically with the influx of young people from the entertainment industry and the world of fashion. As a photographer in the fifties, Beaton felt to some extent an outsider in high society, although he wanted to be accepted, and his diaries are full of references to its members.

Margaret, Duchess of Argyll, was a typical socialite and Beaton describes her in 1955 as 'one of the few left today who still feels impervious to the approach of the common

'Oh, to hell with Nancy Mitford! What I always say is – if it's *me* it's U!' (*1.5.56*)

13 Osbert Lancaster cartoon, 1956, which made fun of Nancy Mitford's methods of distinguishing 'U' (Upper Class) and 'Non-U' behaviour patterns.

man. Her money has given her a sense of security. . .'

I'm a very good housekeeper . . . I talk to my cook on the house telephone each morning, but I woudn't dream of going down to the kitchen. She knows that I can't boil an egg, so what can I tell her? I hate it in America where nowadays your hostess puts on an apron and says she is going to fry a steak. . . (Duchess of Argyll, talking to Beaton).

Clarissa Churchill, who married Anthony Eden, was an old friend of Beaton's. He wrote:

Whenever I met her husband, a wave of what I had hoped was long-forgotten shyness would again overwhelm me. Anthony, by nature, himself is shy, Clarissa too. So we made an agonizing trio: three people, all wanting to be nice to one another, stumbling about in the mire. (July 1951.)

Beaton was present when Winston

14 Coronation of Queen Elizabeth II in 1953. Cecil Beaton had a seat in the Abbey.

Churchill gave a party in 1955, prior to his retirement as Prime Minister. He describes Churchill as looking

smaller than one remembered. A cigar was held in tapering pink fingers, and he wore a look of acute amusement in his eyes.

Other guests included Lady Violet Bonham Carter, Cynthia Asquith, Sir Archibald Sinclair, Diana Cooper, and the Romilly and Mitford families. Churchill's successor Anthony Eden and his wife were 'conspicuous by their absence'. When asked to make a speech, Winston said, 'My days of speech-

making are almost over. Someone else can do it', and he pointed to Lord Goddard. 'Why not he who sends bad men to the gallows.' Churchill complained bitterly to Beaton about the portrait Graham Sutherland had recently painted of him. 'These modern chaps! You're in their power.'

Beaton's costume designs for *My Fair Lady* were his greatest theatrical triumph during the fifties. The musical opened in April 1958 and starred Julie Andrews and Rex Harrison. Cathleen Nesbitt, who played Mrs Higgins, wrote: 'When I heard I was to be dressed by

15 Cecil Beaton in 1959.

Cecil Beaton, I really wouldn't have minded having no lines at all' (Nesbitt, *A Little Love and Good Company*). The film version, starring Audrey Hepburn and Rex Harrison, came out in 1964 and Beaton received two Oscars for his work. The costumes he designed for *Gigi* in 1957 also thrilled audiences.

Beaton's name often appeared in lists of best-dressed men, although his clothes were sometimes outrageous. When discussing Teddy Boys with Nancy Mitford, Evelyn Waugh described them as being dressed like Beaton in 'braided trousers and velvet collars' (Mark Amory (ed.), *Letters to Evelyn Waugh*.) Beaton had worked for *Vogue* since before the war, and when his contract expired in 1955, Harry Yoxall, British Managing Director, wrote: 'Cecil was an inspiring collaborator. He was the only one who was able to write, draw and photograph. He made, I think, a greater contribution to the reputation of *Vogue* than any other artist.'

When Cecil Beaton was given a CBE in 1956 he wrote to Eden, 'I was quite taken aback that I should have been thought of in connection with any honour as the sort of work I do doesn't seem to fit into any of the accepted categories.' He was given a knighthood in 1972. Beaton's photography, like that of his contemporaries Norman Parkinson and John French, involved re-touching and soft focus and was very different from the unvarnished authenticity of photographers like David Bailey, who became the idols of the sixties.

THE SHADOW OF THE BOMB

The 1950s were uneasy years for British foreign policy. War-time co-operation with Russia had been replaced by Cold War and open hostilities seemed likely to break out at any time. Berlin, which had been divided between the Allied Powers as a result of the war, was always a trouble-spot and tension reached a head in 1961 when the Russians built a wall dividing the city. There was a another dangerously volatile situation in Korea, where in 1950 the Communist North had attacked the non-Communist, USA-supported South. Although in every sense of the word a war, an outright confrontation did not take place between the two blocs as the United Nations sent out forces ostensibly to keep the peace. Mainly American troops fought in Korea, supported by the British, but the war was a heavy drain on Britain's budget. Although after Stalin's death in 1953 there was a more moderate regime in Russia, the brutal suppression of the Hungarian Revolution in 1956 by the Russians emphasized the division between the two blocs.

One of the consequences of Cold War was an American paranoia about spies, which culminated in Senator McCarthy's witch hunts of supposed Communists in the early fifties. The extent to which Communists had infiltrated the British Secret Service was only revealed much later. The first scandal was in 1950, when an atomic research expert, Dr Klaus Fuchs, was arrested and given a 14-year sentence for passing information to Russia. A few months later another Harwell scientist, Dr Bruno Pontecorvo, disappeared and was later found to be employed in the Soviet Union. Fuchs' testimony resulted in the trial in America of Julius and Ethel Rosenberg, the first US civilians to be executed for espionage. Investigations in Britain led to the defection of the diplomats Burgess and Maclean, who had been 'moles' since the 1930s.

People were very conscious of the threat of nuclear war in the fifties. The first American hydrogen bomb was exploded in 1952, followed by an improved version detonated on Bikini Atoll in 1954. The Russians retaliated with their own H-Bomb. Britain was determined to develop her own nuclear weapons in order to maintain her status as a world power and tested an H-Bomb in 1957. The Prime Minister, Harold Macmillan, said:

When the tests are completed we shall be in the same position as the United States or Soviet Russia. . . It will be possible then to discuss on equal terms.

16 Hydrogen bomb detonated by the United States on the Marshall Islands in 1952.

17 The Gloucestershire Regiment at Church Parade in Korea, shortly before the historic battle of the Imjin River in 1951, where their commander, Lt Colonel James Carne, won a VC. Many National Servicemen took part in the action.

The Labour Opposition was divided on the issue and Aneurin Bevan urged his party not to let the Foreign Minister go 'naked into the international conference chamber'. In fact after the Suez disaster in 1956 it had become clear that Britain was no longer a world power and would need American help in order to contain Russia. There was also by this time growing opposition to the nuclear arms race and the nuclear disarmament movement was born in Britain, the first protest march to Aldermaston taking place at Easter 1958.

Men in uniform were still a common sight in the fifties, as a peacetime army was needed to fulfil British commitments all over the world. Under the National Service Act of 1948 all young men had to serve up to two years in the forces and National Service was not abolished until 1964. There was also the Z Reserve, consisting of veterans from the war who retrained in camp for a fortnight each year and were called back for service when necessary. There was even a Home Guard, which was re-formed in 1951.

18 Hungarian children, who arrived in Britain with their parents as refugees after the Hungarian Uprising in 1956.

Anthony Eden (1897-1977)

When he succeeded Winston Churchill as Prime Minister in April 1955, Anthony Eden already had a distinguished career behind him as Foreign Secretary to succeeding Conservative governments since 1935. Eden had fought in World War I and afterwards studied Oriental languages at Oxford, entering Parliament for the first time in 1923. He had resigned as Foreign Secretary in 1938 as a protest against the Munich Agreement but had been called back to serve in Churchill's war cabinet. When the Conservatives beat Labour in the 1951 election, he again became Foreign Secretary. By this time Churchill was old and frail and it was clear that Eden would be his successor.

As Foreign Secretary in the early fifties Eden wished to protect his country's position in the world. He did not want Britain to be part of a United Europe, nor did he wish her to be dominated by the United States. There were differences with the Americans in 1951, as Eden wished to limit Premier Mohammad Mosaddeq's power in Iran which was endangering British oil interests, whereas the American President, Harry S. Truman, wanted to give him financial support. The situation in Egypt also caused concern, as nationalists were demanding British withdrawal from the Canal Zone (held under the 1936 Anglo-Egyptian treaty) and from the Sudan (subject to an Act of 1899). When the Egyptian King Farouk was replaced by the more liberal General Neguib, Eden opened negotiations with the new regime. In the same period he helped to resolve differences between Italy and Yugoslavia over ownership of Trieste, meeting President Tito of Yugoslavia to discuss the problems and inviting him to visit Britain in 1953.

Between 1952 and 1953 two major events occurred in Eden's private life. The first was his marriage to Clarissa Churchill in 1952. Publicity was favourable in spite of the differences in the couple's ages and the fact that Eden was divorced. The second was that he was beginning to suffer from jaundice and was told in 1953 that he would need a gall-bladder operation. It was then that a tragic accident took place. During the operation his biliary duct was accidentally cut, necessitating more operations and what would result in bad health for the rest of his life. While he was convalescent Churchill, who had temporarily taken over responsibility for Foreign Affairs, made a speech in the Commons asking for a summit meeting with America and Russia, now that Stalin was dead. Eden was furious and believed that the speech had done untold damage to Britain's relations with Europe.

19 Prime Minister Churchill with his Foreign Secretary Anthony Eden greeting John Foster Dulles of the USA in 1954. Dulles later became a bitter opponent of Eden's policy during the Suez Crisis.

While Eden had been away in America in 1953 for another operation, Churchill suffered a mild stroke. The news was kept secret as the Prime Minister did not feel that R.A. Butler, the other possible candidate for office, was ready for the job. By the time that Eden returned, Churchill had almost completely recovered and did not resign for another two years. During this time Eden had to work with an increasingly aged and difficult Prime Minister, knowing it was rumoured that Churchill was holding on to power because he had little confidence in Eden as his successor.

In 1954 there were more problems with the Americans when Eden refused to back their support of the French in Indo-China – an action which he felt might have resulted in war with China. At the Geneva Conference, which took place that year, Eden helped to secure an armistice in which Vietnam was to be divided at the seventeenth parallel. Churchill had not been happy about the deterioration in relations with America and was also opposed to Eden's plan for the gradual withdrawal of British forces in Suez. However by the end of 1954 Eden had negotiated a compromise agreement with Neguib's successor, Colonel Nasser, guaranteeing British evacuation of the Canal Zone within 20 months, the retention of a British base for seven years and freedom of navigation through the Canal. During this remarkable year for British foreign policy the oil crisis in Iran was also resolved and Eden took part in negotiations through which Germany became a full member of NATO and Britain guaranteed to provide forces for the defence of Europe.

Meanwhile Churchill continued to urge for a meeting with the Russians, leading to a quarrel with his Foreign Secretary during which 'Eden got red in the face with anger and there was a disagreeable scene', according to eye-witness Sir John Colville. Disagreements between the couple became worse and Churchill's eightieth birthday passed without his expected retirement. When in 1955 a new leader, Kruschev, replaced Malenkov in Russia, the Prime Minister again tried to arrange a Summit meeting. In April of that year Churchill at last reluctantly agreed to retire and Eden became Prime Minister, calling at once a General Election to confirm his position.

Once in power, it soon became clear to his colleagues that he lacked confidence and had little experience in dealing with home affairs. Churchill's project, a visit to Britain of the Russian leaders Bulganin and Kruschev, was moderately successful, but in July 1956 the event occurred which was to overshadow Eden's whole career – Nasser nationalized the Suez Canal. President Eisenhower in America advised caution, but Eden found more belligerent allies in the French and Israelis. Action commenced with an Israeli attack on Sinai on 29 October 1956, followed by Anglo-French bombing and a landing on

5 November. The United Nations, led by the Americans, condemned the action and Eden agreed to a cease-fire and the replacement of Anglo-French troops by United Nations forces.

Eden's act – incomprehensible to many, as he had already agreed to negotiate Britain's withdrawal from the Canal Zone – caused divisions in the Government and Commonwealth, a loss of British prestige in the Middle East and endangered world peace. The Anglo-American alliance had also been split and the West's attention had been taken away from the Hungarian Uprising, which had broken out at the same time and was quickly suppressed by the Russians. The British United Nations representative, Sir Pierson Dixon, noted in his diary:

I remember feeling very strongly that we had by our action reduced ourselves from a first-class to a third-class power. . . .

The crisis was debated in Britain in the newspapers, in offices and in people's homes. As Robert Rhodes James has written, 'Like Munich, it divided families and broke long friendships' (*Anthony Eden*).

Although Eden believed that he had made the right decision, his health was broken by Suez and he retired in January 1957 on medical advice. In his retirement he wrote four books and died in 1977. He had worked for most of his career under the shadow of

21 Rally held in Trafalgar Square, London, to protest against Government action in the Suez Crisis, November 1956. The meeting was addressed by the Labour leader Aneurin Bevan.

Winston Churchill and unfairly his name is now associated with Suez, rather than with the skill and dedication he showed during his years as Foreign Secretary.

Guy Burgess (1911-63) and Donald Maclean (1913-1983)

The defection to Russia in 1951 of Guy Burgess and Donald Maclean, the two men known to the press as 'The Missing Diplomats', was a severe blow to the British Secret Service and to the Establishment generally, who could not believe that members of their own class had 'let the side down' so badly. Their story was read eagerly

22   The 'Missing Diplomat' Donald Maclean with his daughter, shortly before his defection to Moscow.

by members of the public and became a long running saga as more moles in the Secret Service were unmasked over the next 35 years.

Both men came from middle-class backgrounds. Burgess's father was a vicar and he had gone to school at Marlborough. Maclean's father was a Liberal MP and a lawyer, and he had been to Eton. Both were at Cambridge in the 1930s during a time of mass unemployment, when the rise of fascism in Europe was causing alarm. After Labour's defeat in the 1931 election some thought Communism was the only way to fight fascism and lead Britain out of the slump. Both men were recruited to the party whilst at Cambridge.

Like Kim Philby and Anthony Blunt, also recruited at Cambridge in the same period, they never made any secret of the fact that they were Marxists whilst at university. Burgess, Maclean and Blunt had the additional link of belonging to an elitist society known as 'The Apostles', some of whose members, like themselves, were homosexuals – a criminal offence at that time, and another link which

bound them together in conspiracy. Of the four, Kim Philby was the most valuable to the Russians, first as head of the anti-Soviet department of MI6 after the war, and later as liaison officer in Washington with the CIA and the FBI. He was in fact in line for being made head of MI6 when the Foreign Office put in an adverse report, saying that he was drinking too much and clearly unsuitable for such an important post.

Donald Maclean entered the Diplomatic Service in 1935 after leaving university and was posted to Paris, where he married his wife Melinda. His subsequent career took him to Washington and Cairo, and he was made a Counsellor at the early age of 35. Meanwhile Burgess, who had first joined the BBC, did not enter the Foreign Office until 1944, when he became a temporary press officer in the News Department. He was made an established member of the Foreign Office in 1947 and worked for a time for the Minister of State Hector McNeil, and in the Far Eastern Department. Although not in such a good position for classified information as Maclean, Burgess had a wide circle of friends in high places and through informal gatherings in his flat was able to find out much which was of interest to the Russians.

The Americans first voiced suspicions about Maclean in 1949 whilst he was in Cairo, when the FBI managed to crack a code used to relay messages from the Russian consulate in New York to Moscow between 1944 and 1945. Evidence pointed to a spy at the British consulate who had knowledge of phone calls between Churchill and President Truman, and Maclean was one of the suspects. He was warned by Burgess that his cover had been broken, and anxiety, coupled with alcohol, caused him to be sent back to London in May 1950 suffering from a 'nervous breakdown'. According to Philip Knightley, writing in *The Second Oldest Profession*, Maclean was accustomed at this time to buttonhole people when he was drunk saying things like 'Buy me a drink. I'm the English Hiss' (Alger Hiss: a US State Department official who passed information to Russia) or 'I'm working for Uncle Joe' (Stalin).

Burgess, too, could be highly indiscreet. He was a heavy drinker and had numerous homosexual contacts. Indeed both he and Maclean were becoming liabilities to the Russians as well as to the British. Unaccountably the couple were able to brazen the situation out for another year. Maclean was given a home posting in October 1950 as Head of the American Department of the Foreign Office and Burgess was sent as Second Secretary to Washington.

The way in which the defection of Burgess and Maclean took place was a shock for the British but also something of a blunder by the KGB. Suspicion would fall on Kim Philby and Anthony Blunt if a case was proved against Burgess, but Philby, who was in Washington at the time, must have panicked and suggested the unsuitable Burgess as the agent for getting Maclean away. Perhaps at his own instigation, Burgess was sent home in disgrace to England because of a traffic offence in America. Hearing that Maclean's interrogation by the Secret Service was scheduled for 28 May 1951, Burgess went to warn him at his home and the two vanished on the evening of 25 May for the next five years. In the original Russian plan Burgess was not meant to accompany Maclean and his impulsive action put the pressure particularly on Blunt, a close friend who had shared a home with him during the war. Maclean's wife and children followed him to Russia in 1953, managing to elude both the press and the Secret Service.

23 Guy Burgess, who defected with Donald Maclean, with Express reporter Terry Lancaster in Moscow, 1957. The picture was sent from Moscow by wire – which caused the distortions.

The story of the vanishing diplomats was the press sensation of the year, and an embarrassment for the Labour government which had at that time only a small majority. The Americans were particularly infuriated by British mismanagement of the affair. The hunt was now on for a 'Third Man', who had given the tip-off about Maclean's interrogation and although Philby was under suspicion for the next seven years by MI5, there were many who thought he had been treated badly and was being penalized for his left-wing sympathies whilst at university. He was forced to resign from MI6 in 1952 and became a journalist in Beirut, and may even have retained links with his old office. He too finally escaped to Russia in 1963, when British intelligence had gathered sufficient evidence to indict him. It was not until 1979 that the case against Blunt became public, although he had made a confession to security officers in 1964.

One of the results of the Burgess and Maclean affair was that the old trust that the Establishment placed in people of middle-class academic and social background was broken. The two spies were given accommodation and jobs in Moscow and later had some personal contact with their friends and families. They did not appear to be as happy there as Philby, and Burgess tried many times to return to Britain on a visit.

24 Osbert Lancaster cartoon in 1951 referring to the 'Missing Diplomats' — the case was the press sensation of the year.

'Now why on earth, darling, should you think it's either Burgess or Maclean? For all you know it's just as likely to be our host.' (*19.7.51*)

Leslie Thomas (1931-   )

Leslie Thomas was a National Serviceman in the early fifties and afterwards wrote a book based on his experiences called *The Virgin Soldiers*, which later became a successful film. Born in Wales in 1931, he was brought up in a Barnado's orphanage after his parents died during the war. In his autobiography he describes how keen he was to get into the Army, which

was only matched, after a short period in uniform, by my eagerness to get out again. (*In My Wildest Dreams.*)

He was no exception to the rule (and constant complaint of ex-National Servicemen) that the army did not use his civilian skills. Having given his profession as 'junior reporter', he was put in the Royal Army Pay Corps – only discovering later that he had been recorded as a 'junior porter'. On reflection he decided that his posting could have been worse.

The first day for recruits was generally a shock. After being issued with their Pay Book and Soldier's Service Book, they were given the traditional 'short back and sides' haircut. A medical followed and then kits was issued. Thomas, whose first posting was Devizes, said 'we went around like cardboard men in the new, stiff, ill-fitting battledress'. During 'basic training' everything was done at the double.

We pounded up and down the barrack square, shouting out the time of the movements like chorus girls; our feet emerging with howling blisters from boots stiff as tombstones.

Recruits were put through a comprehensive training for war, including bayonet practice, which Thomas reckoned was unnecessary for a member of the Pay Corps. Men slept 20 to a hut, where class distinctions quickly vanished, only to reappear later if a recruit was selected as a PO (potential officer). Thomas

25 Leslie Thomas (marked with a X) during his National Service days in Singapore.

was amazed how quickly most people adapted and 'began to think and act like regimental robots'.

Another ex-National Serviceman, Lance Corporal R. Dulson, remembers

Basic training was all rush and bull. During the day we were rushed all over the place – shouted at and bullied all the time. Evenings were spent bulling kit and there was very little free time. (Trevor Royale, *The Best Years of Their Lives.*)

Basic training over, Leslie Thomas was instructed in army accounts – a month of excruciating boredom, he recalls – and then came the Passing-Out Parade, after which recruits dispersed to their various units. Thomas was posted to the Regimental Pay Office at Whitchurch, Hampshire, and after a short while was put on a draft for Singapore.

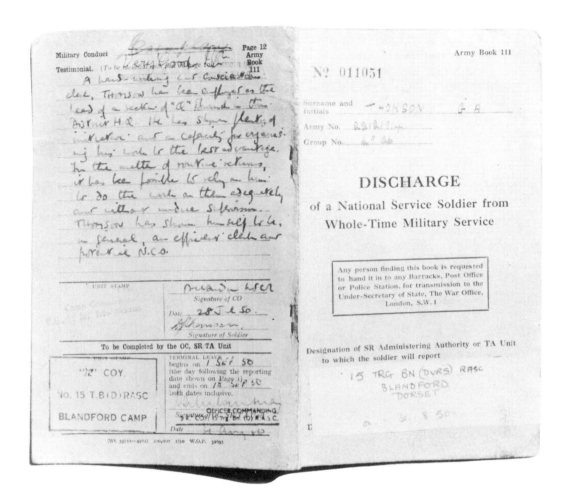

26 Army Discharge Papers belonging to a National Serviceman.

After a 35-day journey by sea he arrived at his new barracks, which had previously been a Japanese prisoner of war camp. The war had effectively marked the end of power for the British in Malaya. When they returned after the Japanese occupation they had the Communist Malay Races Liberation Army to contend with, and a state of emergency had been in operation there since 1948.

In spite of its dangers Malaya was not an unpopular posting, as it also had beaches and the exotic nightlife of Singapore as compensations. Thomas was transferred to the section which dealt with the paybooks of casualties and came to realize the number of National Servicemen, as well as regulars, who were killed in the jungle. Soon afterwards he was posted up-country to Mersing for active

duty. The camp was in the jungle in close proximity to a bandit hide-out. Soldiers were on guard duty every other night and during the day went into the jungle on patrol.

Leslie Thomas was expecting to be demobilized after the 18 months he had signed on for, but the period of service was extended to two years as the Korean War had broken out. 'Z' Reservists were also called back and Thomas describes a meeting with an elderly officer in Singapore who said

I thought . . . that when the war was finished it was *finished*. . . And then they come around and tell me that I've got to go back in the army because I'm a reservist. I never knew they could get you back just like that.

When Thomas was finally discharged the Army did not provide any civilian clothes as they had done after the war. Men were, however, allowed to keep their uniform as they were still on the reserve. Thomas went on to become a Fleet Street reporter and writer.

A compulsory two years in the Forces had a profound effect on the young men of the period. Among the many books that were written based on their experiences were David Lodge's *Ginger, You're Barmy* and Alan Sillitoe's *Key to the Door*. Gordon Williams's *The Camp* described National Service in the RAF, as did Arnold Wesker's play *Chips with Everything*. Many of the men remember the friends they made and the feeling of growing up fast. One ex-serviceman, quoted in *The Best Years of Their Lives*, believes that

My service gave me self-confidence, taught me comradeship, understanding of my fellow men, discipline and an appreciation of my home and parents. I returned to Caernarvon a very responsible adult.

On the other hand, some found the experience disrupting, and had difficulty picking up their careers when they got back. The rest of the population grew accustomed to seeing their sons and boyfriends in uniform long after the war was over.

OUTSIDERS AND ANGRY YOUNG MEN

During the decade following World War II British culture was conservative and established pre-war writers like J.B. Priestley, C.P. Snow and Cyril Connolly dominated the literary scene. Malcolm Bradbury, graduate from a provincial university, was told he was less likely to get his work published than his contemporaries at Oxbridge (interview in *A Look Back to Anger*, Radio 4, 22 December 1987.) Readers of the Socialist *New Statesman* complained that reviews of the Arts appeared to be written by Conservatives. The theatre was London oriented and its most popular playwrights – Terence Rattigan, T.S. Eliot, Noel Coward and Christopher Fry – all wrote with an upper-middle class audience in mind.

The British cinema was led by Ealing Studios, whose films poked gentle fun at British life from a middle-class standpoint. There was film and theatre censorship and publishers could be prosecuted for obscenity – the most notorious example being the case against Penguin Books for republishing D.H. Lawrence's *Lady Chatterley's Lover* in 1959.

A long overdue reaction against traditional British cultural values occurred in the mid-fifties, partly as a result of Continental and American influences. The ideas developed in Colin Wilson's book *The Outsider* (1956) owed much to the French existentialist philosopher Jean-Paul Sartre. Wilson's brand of existentialism offered a cure for society through the Outsider or Superman, who would guide humanity towards a better world. His book became a best-seller but had little lasting influence. However, the idea of the Outsider in its non-philosophical sense caught the imagination of young people, who identified with American teenage heroes, film stars Marlon Brando and James Dean, who portrayed characters fighting a world of conformity.

27 Typical British film in 1955, starring Norman Wisdom – before the 'Angry' movement.

28 Colin Wilson, whose book *The Outsider* became a best-seller in 1956. Wilson claimed to have written the book while sleeping rough on Hampstead Heath.

A number of young writers appeared during the early fifties, who were unconnected with each other but had sufficient similarities for the press to group them together as 'Angry Young Men' – a title drived from a character in John Osborne's play *Look Back in Anger*, first performed in 1956. Kingsley Amis's *Lucky Jim* (1954) describes the adventures of a grammar school educated ex-serviceman, now lecturing at a provincial university, who challenges upper class attitudes at every opportunity. The hero of Amis's second book *That Uncertain Feeling* (1955) also declares himself 'a sworn foe of the bourgeois'. Although *Lucky Jim* described life in a provincial university, Amis had in fact been to Oxford. Later Malcolm Bradbury noticed that although an admiration of provincial 'red-brick' universities was usual among 'angry' writers of the fifties, not many had been there themselves. Bradbury, who was at Leicester university, found students eager to conform, 'passing on into teaching or business seemingly untouched by what the university stood for – whatever that was' (*Eating People is Wrong*, 1959.)

29 Kingsley Amis, the author of *Lucky Jim* (1954).

Novelists John Braine and John Wain were also prominent among the 'Angries'. Wain's *Hurry on Down* (1953) tells the story of a university dropout's efforts to make a living and John Braine's *Room at the Top* (1957) describes self-educated Joe Lampton's unscrupulous attempts to get a top job and top girl in a North country town. Joe despises the 'world of worry about rent and rates and groceries'. He wants the status symbols 'an Aston-Martin . . . a three-guinea linen shirt . . . a girl with a Riviera suntan'. Other novelists who shared some of the Angry Young Men's characteristics included Alan Sillitoe (*Saturday Night and Sunday Morning*, 1958), Keith Waterhouse (*Billy Liar*, 1959) and Stan Barstow (*A Kind of Loving*, 1960). At first the literary establishment looked down on the new writers as cultural Teddy Boys, but they expressed views which were waiting to be said and appealed particularly to the young.

A similar reaction against current attitudes to film led to the Free Cinema movement. Its leaders – Lindsay Anderson, Tony Richardson and Karel Reisz – believed 'in the importance of people and in the significance of the everyday'. They thought that no genuine working class films had been made in Britain and that the British, unlike the French, had never taken the cinema seriously. The subject matter of their documentaries included an evening at a jazz club (*Momma Don't Allow*), a night at Covent Garden Market (*Every Day Except Christmas*) and an impression of a seaside amusement park (*O Dreamland*). The films were not widely seen at the time, but the directors went on in the sixties to make feature films like Lindsay Anderson's *This Sporting Life* (1963) and Karel Reisz's *Saturday Night and Sunday Morning* which incorporated their Free Cinema principles.

There were other Outsiders who had more serious problems during the period. These were the immigrants, who were arriving in large numbers from Africa and the West Indies – over 30,000 of them between 1954 and '55. The majority were men between 20 and 35 who found jobs with public transport or in the mines. Many encountered prejudice and intolerance and those with higher qualifications found it almost impossible to get work. They settled in districts near their friends and the first race riots occurred in Nottingham and Notting Hill Gate in 1958.

John Osborne (1929-   )

When John Osborne's play *Look Back in Anger* opened at the Royal Court Theatre in May 1956 it was described by Kenneth Tynan in *The Observer* as showing

post-war youth as it really is, with special emphasis on the non-U intelligentsia . . . a minor miracle. All the qualities are there, qualities one had despaired of ever seeing on the stage . . . the best young play of its decade.

T.C. Worsley saw in it 'the authentic new tone of the nineteen-fifties, desperate, savage, resentful and, at times, very funny'. (*New Statesman*.) Although at the time he was considered the leading spokesman of his generation, Osborne's work was intensely personal and based on his own very real hatred of middle-class society, in contrast with Kingsley Amis, who generally mocked his enemies with affection.

Osborne's early life was spent in the London suburbs, where he developed a burning resentment of his mother's middle-class pretensions. After his father's death he was given an assisted place at a minor public

30 John Osborne (right) and Kenneth Haigh – author and star of *Look Back in Anger* – standing outside the Royal Court Theatre in London, where the play was produced by the English Stage Company. The Company became well-known for sponsoring new talents in the late fifties and sixties.

school, from which he was expelled in 1945 after punching the headmaster. His first job was in publishing, but after dabbling in amateur dramatics he was taken on as an assistant stage manager by a repertory company. While working as an actor with another company in the early fifties he met and married actress Pamela Lane. He began to write plays – among them *Epitaph for George Dillon*, which was not performed until 1958.

Soon after his marriage broke up, Osborne saw an advertisement in *The Stage* saying that the newly-formed English Stage Company was looking for plays by new writers. George Devine, the Artistic Director, was enthusiastic about *Look Back in Anger* and the play was produced a year later.

Look Back in Anger had its roots in John Osborne's personal relationships and social background. In his autobiography *A Better Class of Person* he admits that Jimmy Porter's description of his marriage to Alison was 'a fairly accurate description' of his wedding to Pamela Lane. The Lanes had been against the marriage and at one stage had hired private detectives to see if a scandal about him could be discovered. As Osborne had written the play soon after the breakdown of his marriage, his fury against Pamela Lane's parents is incorporated in the play. Jimmy says

There is no limit to what the middle-aged mummy will do in the holy crusade against ruffians like me. . . Threatened with me, a young man without money, background or even looks, she'd bellow like a rhinoceros in labour.

Throughout the play Jimmy Porter rants noisily against his unresponsive wife Alison – a pitiful character constantly at the ironing board – his dislikes encompassing the Church of England, the Sunday papers, the upper

31 Scene from *Look Back in Anger*, showing the down-trodden Alison (Mary Ure) ironing while Jimmy (Kenneth Haigh) and Cliff (Alan Bates) play the fool.

classes, the Americanization of Britain and his wife's relations. As Alison explains to her friend Helena, Jimmy works on a sweet stall in the market because they had no money, no job and no home after they were married.

He'd only left the university about a year. (*Smiles.*) No -left. I don't think one 'comes down' from Jimmy's university. According to him, it's not even red brick, but white tile.

Osborne's next play, *The Entertainer*, opened in May 1957. Sir Laurence Olivier played the leading character, a failed comedian called Archie Rice. Archie tells his daughter 'look at my eyes. I'm dead behind these eyes. I'm dead, just like the whole inert, shoddy lot out there.' He is the product of a public school which 'produced one Field Marshall with strong Fascist tendencies, one Catholic poet who went bonkers and Archie Rice'. Osborne wrote the play during the Suez Crisis and many of his bitter comments caused noisy reactions among the theatre audiences. When Archie's son Mick is killed in the Canal Zone (the other, a conscientious objector, stokes hospital boilers) his daughter says at the funeral

Why do people like us sit here, and just lap it all up, why do boys die, or stoke boilers, why do we pick up these things, what are we hoping to get out of it, what's it all in aid of – is it really just for the sake of a gloved hand waving at you from a golden coach?

John Osborne went on to write *The World of Paul Slickey* (1959), with a gossip columnist as hero. According to John Russell Taylor (*Anger and After*) the play attacks with equal fury

the church, the aristocracy, the gutter Press, those masculine women and feminine men (as well as their more bigoted opponents), the success ethos, the tawdriness of teenage tastes in music, the sentimentality of the woman's magazine, supporters of blood sports and corporal punishment, anti-semites, anti-negroes, and anti-anti-H-bomb demonstrators, and just about every other imaginable *bête noire* of the discontented intellectual. . .

John Osborne's generation, born in the late twenties or early thirties, had seen poverty and unemployment, followed by war and the atom bomb. They had enthusiastically voted Labour in the 1945 election but were disillusioned because the brave new world for which they were hoping had not materialized. Many were ex-Servicemen who had been given Government grants to go to university. Becoming students again did not always suit them. They were anxious to finish their training quickly and get jobs, and certainly had no patience with the Oxbridge Establishment, who still had the power to thwart their ambitions in private as well as public life.

Many grammar school educated graduates from working-class families felt rootless – guilty because their education had cut them off from their parents and angry because it had not given them the social and business success for which they had hoped. The post-atom bomb generations identified with Jimmy Porter, when he said in *Look Back in Anger*

I suppose people of our generation aren't able to die for good causes any longer. We had all that done for us, in the thirties and the forties, when we were still kids. There aren't any good, brave causes left. If the big bang does come, and we all get killed off, it won't be in aid of the old-fashioned, grand design. [It will be as] pointless and inglorious as stepping in front of a bus.

John Osborne's private beliefs were perhaps more widely held than he had realized.

Colin MacInnes (1914-76)

Colin MacInnes was the son of the novelist Angela Thirkell and related to Stanley Baldwin and Rudyard Kipling. He was born in Australia, but lived for most of his life in London, where he wrote about the young, the poor, the immigrants and the criminals – all outsiders in their way, but with their own complicated customs and beliefs. As a homosexual – which was illegal at that time – MacInnes felt he was also an outsider, and was able to get under the skin of those who did not conform. He was older than the other literary rebels and was never grouped with the Angry Young Men. He thought of himself as an explorer who interpreted different aspects of society. Writing in *The Spectator* in 1961, Bernard Levin remarked,

Until quite recently I believed . . . that Mr Colin MacInnes was a black man. . . The trouble is that having read *England, Half English* I am rather more inclined to believe that I was right all the time. . . He is not merely a reporter, a chronicler; he is an analyst, and one of extraordinary range and power. . . .

32 The author and journalist Colin MacInnes.

After leaving the Army in 1946 MacInnes became Art Critic for *The Observer* for a short time. Later he joined the BBC radio programme, *The Critics*. The bulk of his writing was done in the fifties and early sixties and his books included *To The Victor The Spoils* (1950), *June in her Spring* (1952), *City of Spades* (1957), *Absolute Beginners* (1959), *Mr Love and Justice* (1960) and *England Half English* (1961). He also wrote numerous articles in newspapers and periodicals. His friends remember him with affection, although his personal habits sometimes made him a difficult guest. Ray Gosling says, 'Colin lent me money, got me into and out of many

scrapes' (*Personal Copy*). George Melly recalls,

However much we may have dreaded finding that tall, good-looking, casually elegant, sardonic figure on the doorstep determined to take up as much of our time as he chose and probably insult us at the end of it, we all learnt a lot from him (*The Observer* 1985.)

MacInnes became obsessed with London sub-cultures during the fifties, in particular that of the immigrants. His novel *City of Spades* describes the adventures of Johnny Fortune, a black immigrant from Lagos, in the seedier parts of London. The book contains many sharp insights about immigrant society – the differences between Africans and West Indians, problems with landlords, difficulties of making a living, relationships with white women – all contained within a exuberant, amusing novel. It is quite easy to imagine, like Bernard Levin, that the writer is a black man. The whites ('Jumbles') in the novel are generally unsympathetic, like the old man in a pub who wants to know how Spades (black men) know 'which is African, and which is West Indian'. To this Johnny replies, '. . . my grandmother cannot tell any one Englishman from another'. Detective-Inspector Purity of the Yard complains,

First the Maltese come, then the Cypriots, and now this lot! They don't make the copper's task any the easier.

Colin MacInnes demonstrates the differences between African and West Indian immigrants in *City of Spades* and other publications. In the fifties the Africans were generally seamen, students or traders. Some

were propelled here by a *wanderlust* that possessed so many Africans. . . The case of the West Indians is much simpler: they have always been an emigrating people . . . a young West Indian (like an Irishman half a century or more ago) must seek his fortune elsewhere to prosper, even to survive. ('Britain's Half-Million' from *Africa South in Exile*, Vol. 5, No. 2, 1961.)

33 This man arrived in Birmingham from Jamaica in the mid-1950s trained as a radio technician, but could only find work as a bus conductor. His story was a typical one.

The West Indians felt they were English. As Mr Tamberlain, a character in *City of Spades* put it,

Our islands is colonies of great antiquity, and our mother tongue is English, like your own. . . So naturally we expect you treat us like we're British as yourself, and when you don't, we suffer and go sour.

Africans, on the other hand,

speak their own private tongues, their lives are rooted in their ancient tribes, so that even when they're lonely or miserable here they feel they're sustained by the solid tribal past at home.

Absolute Beginners is packed with information about the teenage scene in London during the late fifties – coffee bars, Vespas, jazz clubs, disc shops 'with those lovely sleeves . . . the most original thing to come out in our lifetime'. The unnamed hero is an 18-year-old photographer living in Notting Hill Gate, which he likes for its sleaziness and because people there accept you for what you are. He is a sharp dresser:

grey pointed alligator casuals, the pink neon pair of ankle crepe nylon-stretch, my Cambridge blue glove-fit jeans, a vertical-striped happy shirt revealing my lucky neck-charm on its chain. . . .

He likes jazz clubs because

no one, not a soul, cares what your class is, or what your race is, or what your income, or if you're a boy, or girl, or bent, or versatile, or what you are – so long as you dig the scene. . . .

The book ends with the Notting Hill race riots, when the hero identifies with the blacks. He says,

In the history books, they tell us the English race has spread itself all over the world. . . No one invited us, and we didn't ask anyone's permission, I suppose. Yet when a few hundred thousand come and settle among our fifty millions, we just can't take it.

Colin MacInnes did his best work in the fifties and sixties. Although he continued writing until his death, nothing had the immediacy, insight and pace of his novels *City of Spades* and *Absolute Beginners*.

34 The first race riots at Notting Hill Gate, 1958, started by white youths. MacInnes describes how violence was confined to a very small area '. . . across one single road, like some national frontier – you were back in the world of *Mrs Dale*, and *What's My Line* and 'England's green and pleasant land' (*Absolute Beginners*).

E(dward) R(ichard) Braithwaite (1922-   )

Whereas Colin MacInnes interpreted the life of black immigrants to Britain in the fifties, E.R. Braithwaite wrote from experience. He was one of a number of well-educated blacks, many of whom were ex-Servicemen, who tried to make a living in Britain after the war. The problems of the educated were as bad as those of the uneducated, as V.S. Naipaul proved in *The Enigma of Arrival* (1987). Braithwaite was brought up in British Guyana and obtained scholarship to Cambridge University. Later he joined the RAF, completing his degree and returning to London once the war was over. He had always thought of himself as British and did not notice signs of discrimination while serving in the RAF. It was only when he tried to get work after the war as a physicist that he found anti-black prejudice. His experiences are told in his autobiographical novel *Reluctant Neighbours* (1972).

Braithwaite spent frustrating months applying for jobs for which he was well-qualified. Again and again he was turned down. 'Surely', he thought, 'they couldn't all have got together and agreed to keep out black scientists.' Then he tried industry.

Now I was resented for what I knew, the way I dressed and spoke. I was an oddity. A black man with a Master's degree and cultured speech who'd flown Spitfires during the war.

Finally he joined the LCC and became a teacher from 1950 to 1957, where he was given one of the toughest classes at an East End Secondary School.

Expecting to have reasonably behaved children, similar to those at school with him in Guyana, Braithwaite found 'rough, untidy, aggressive young adults', who had little interest in being educated. His struggle to teach them in spite of themselves led to his writing *To Sir, With Love* (1959). Using his own methods he first got his pupils' trust and then tried to develop each individual according to his or her potential. The copious notes he made about his classes gave him background for his novel. He even wrote down what his pupils said, which made the book lively and realistic and contributed to its later success as a film starring Sidney Poitier and Judy Geeson.

In 1958 Braithwaite was persuaded to leave teaching and work as advisor to the LCC Child Welfare Department, where he stayed for two

35 E.R. Braithwaite.

36 West Indian immigrants arrive at Victoria Station, London, in 1956, where they are helped by a member of the Salvation Army. 30,000 immigrants were expected in England from the West Indies in 1956 and many experienced difficulty in finding homes and work.

years. At that time the majority of immigrants were male – women and children followed later – and many found it difficult to adapt to British currency, unfamiliar language and different eating habits. Unlike Braithwaite's own case, there were plenty of unskilled jobs available:

In the hospitals. On the buses and trams. As postmen. As garbage collectors and street cleaners. As unskilled building labourers.

One of the greatest problems for immigrants was housing, and racial discrimination forced them out to the worst areas. Part of Braithwaite's job was to arrange foster homes for children in the Council's care, and he had difficulty placing black children. His attempts to put them in white homes met resistance from his colleagues. Finally he decided to give up the job and wrote *To Sir, With Love*. The success of the book meant that he was now asked to write and lecture on various subjects:

On education, on teaching, and on the plight of the black immigrant in Britain. The outsider writing from inside.

E.R. Braithwaite's subsequent career took him to Paris and America and he later became Permanent Representative of Guyana to the United Nations (1967-8) and Guyanan Ambassador to Venezuela (1968-9).

Jazz, Teds And Teenagers

British customs and social institutions which had survived since before the war were swept away in the mid-fifties by young people, who rejected traditional authority. For the first time the young had the economic power to buy clothes, consumer goods and entertainment. As a result, new professions came to the fore, like photography and hairdressing – which were linked with the fashion industry. Nowhere was the revolution more apparent than in the world of music.

Jazz, which had become popular after the war, had, from its nature, always been anarchic and anti-authoritarian. Its exponents were generally ex-servicemen, like Humphrey Lyttleton and George Melly, but its appeal cut across age groups and it was not a youth cult like pop music. Although jazz continued to have a steady following during the fifties, the traditional jazz enthusiasts in particular showing something of the fervour that went with pop music, the youth movement really got going with the advent of Tommy Steele in 1956.

Entertainment in post-war Britain was essentially middle-aged. Lyons teashops and Corner Houses provided staid, cheap places to eat, patronized by all the family. The first casual meeting places catering for the young were Expresso Bars, which started in the early fifties. An article in *Picture Post* describes how one of these cafes was 'crammed to its glass walls with people. Girls in jeans and poodle cuts. Girls in frocks and horse-tail hairdos. . . We sat by the great, gleaming Expresso machine (imported from Milan) and watched this growing transformation in the nation's drinking habits' (21 August 1954). Between 1952 and 1954, 70 new coffee bars had opened in London. Some of them were featuring 'skiffle' players or rock 'n roll stars by the late

fifties. A 16-year-old girl interviewed on the radio in 1958 said,

I think it's best to be a teenager nowadays, because most things are for teenagers. I'm

37 Radiogram for playing records, 1951. The heavy breakable 78s were replaced by plastic 45rpm singles in the mid-fifties and an 'autochange' device enabled a stack of records to be played.

3 SPEED - FOR STANDARD AND LONG PLAYING RECORDS

a complete

RADIOGRAM

for only **30** GNS TAX PAID

dreading to grow old because there's just nothing to do.

A woman interviewed for the BBC's *You'll Never be 16 Again* remembers how she felt when she was a post-war teenager:

You tried to emulate the model look – neat, ladylike and sophisticated. . . I can remember thinking when I was in my teens, "Oh, it must be nice to be 20. . .".

By the mid-fifties teenagers were beginning to show their individuality by their clothes and hairstyles. It was the first time in history that they had money to indulge in their fantasies. The more extreme became Teddy Boys, wearing Edwardian styled clothes and elaborate hairstyles. An article in *Picture Post* entitled 'The Truth about Teddy Boys' described how

The floppy jackets hung to their knees, the poplin shirts were advertisement white, the trousers were ankle tight, the shoes were good black leather, and the ties were narrow bows.

They said, 'Our dress is our answer to a dull world'. (29 May 1954.) Some Teds formed gangs which got into fights and older people often found their image alarming.

Light music on the radio in the early fifties was sentimental and played on programmes like *Housewives' Choice* or *Workers' Playtime*. When Elvis Presley first brought rock 'n roll from America, the BBC would have nothing to do with it. During the fifties old 78 (revolutions per minute) records were replaced by the 'single' 45. Record players – which allowed a stack of records to be played – replaced wind-up gramophones and record sales increased from £3.5 million in 1950 to £15 million by the end of the decade. These two innovations, together with transistor radios and juke-boxes, helped to form teenage taste in music.

38 One of the first Expresso Coffee Bar in London, 1954. The Gaggia machine is in the left foreground. Coffee was drunk from transparent plastic cups.

39 Tommy Steele at the start of his career with some friends in the Bread Basket Coffee House.

George Melly (1926-   )

George Melly discovered jazz while he was at school. When he was demobilized from the Navy after the war, he combined appearances as singer in Mick Mulligan's band with a regular job in an art gallery specializing in surrealist paintings. His autobiography, *Owning Up*, gives a rumbustious account of life on the road with a jazz band in the fifties.

Melly modelled his vocal style on that of American blues singer Bessie Smith, singing with what has been described as 'the raucous charm of an old Negress'. (John Mortimer in *The New Statesman*.) Philip Oakes remembers seeing him do his speciality number, *Frankie and Johnny*,

where he made his death plunge from the edge of the stage to the dance floor, toppling like a felled pine, scattering the dancers as he went. (*At the Jazz Band Ball*.)

He practised these special effects every time he sang the song.

As the band began to get more engagements, Melly left the art gallery. There were several kinds of jazz in Britain during the fifties. The Mulligan Band played New Orleans classics in the style of early Louis Armstrong. Humphrey Lyttleton played 'mainstream', the small band sound of the late thirties and early forties. Ken Colyer was a fundamentalist who tried to recreate the work of musicians like Bunk Johnson, who had never left New Orleans. Fans dressed according to their taste in jazz. Philip Oakes described the Mulligan fans as

ravers who enjoyed the band's music and saw the band itself – raffish, randy and anarchic – as a spearhead in a revolt against years of austerity.

Ken Colyer's fans, often art students and intellectuals, wore their own kind of nonconformist dress – generally black in the case of the girls, who liked to copy the Parisian singer Juliette Greco. In the late fifties Chris Barber converted Ken Colyer's traditional style into something more commercial, starting the Trad jazz boom.

Melly describes jazz as being, the suburbs' escape from their lot. The audience was middle-class and suburban, with a strong element of students, particularly from art schools. Trad was the music of the Aldermaston marchers. (*Revolt into Style.*)

While on tour the Mulligan band played at dance halls and jazz clubs all over the country. Some halls

were luxurious, influenced by the Festival of Britain, given to a wall in a different colour, wallpapers of bamboo poles or grey stones. . . Others were as bare as aeroplane hangers, or last decorated during the early picture palace era.

Lodgings were equally variable. Mrs Flanagan's dining room held a piano

a sideboard with jumbo-sized cornflake packets on it, a looking-glass surrounded by photographs of bandleaders who had stayed there and disfigured by musicians who had worked for them. Soon after her accession, somebody stuck up a postcard of the Queen among the other photographs. On it was written 'Lovely digs, Mrs Flanagan'. It was signed 'Liz and Phil'.

When the Mulligan Band folded in 1953,

40 George Melly, back on the road again with John Chilton and the Feetwarmers, in concert at Kew Gardens, 1987.

41 Dancing to the music of Humphrey Lyttleton and his band at the London Jazz Club.

Melly became a solo singer –

Dressed in a black shirt, black trousers, black socks, black shoes, a very expensive black sweater from Simpsons, and a white silk tie',

with Mick Mulligan as his agent. Mulligan soon wanted to perform again and the band re-formed. Melly met Tommy Steele shortly after his first recordings. On one occasion the Mulligan Band shared a concert billing with Tommy. After seeing the reaction of the girls at the concert to the singer, Frank Parr of the Mulligan Band prophesied,

The death of jazz, rock and roll, the beginning of the end, and he'll have us all in the bread line.

However, jazz retained its following for some years and the Mulligan Band continued until 1961.

Tommy Steele (1936-   )

Rock 'n roll music was an American import. When Bill Haley's film *The Blackboard Jungle*, featuring his song *Rock Around the Clock*, was first shown in London 'the film was stopped for eigheen minutes, in the hope that the uproar among the audience of 900 would subside. . . Young people at the back of the cinema . . . gave vent to their emotion by stretching their arms out to the screen like savages drunk with coconut wine at a tribal sacrifice.' (The *Manchester Guardian*, 10 September 1956.)

Tommy Steele was born at Bermondsey in 1936, leaving school to become a merchant seaman at 15. Soon after leaving his last job on the *Mauretania*, he was spotted singing rock 'n roll in the Two I's coffee bar in Soho and was made into a star immediately. Trevor Philpott wrote; 'Tommy Steele's greatest talent is that he is an ordinary, likeable British kid who obviously gets a kick out of life' (*Picture Post*, 22 February 1957). In a subsequent article he described Steele as

The boy from Bermondsey who woke up one morning to find himself the most screamed-over young man in Europe (4 March 1957).

Steele appeared on television in *Off the Record* on 15 October 1956 and made his stage debut top of the bill at the Sunderland Empire on 5 November the same year. Philpott believed, 'what Tommy is really selling to British youth is Youth itself' and that he would be popular long after the craze for rock 'n roll had died down.

The word used to describe Tommy Steele's music was 'pop', or 'popular'. George Melly describes rock 'n roll fans as

42 Tommy Steele singing rock 'n' roll. Colin MacInnes described him as being 'every nice young girl's boy, every kid's favourite elder brother, every mother's adolescent son.'

working-class and very young. . . Jazz enthusiasts despised rock 'n' roll as musically

43 Fans at a performance by Tommy Steele in 1957. 'At certain ritual gestures . . . the teenagers utter a collective shriek of ectasy. Tommy has *sent* them.' (Colin MacInnes).

illiterate. . . Why this . . . should suddenly have sparked off a whole generation is a mystery. I think it had to do with military service. There was no point in getting on with your life after leaving school and while waiting to be called up. So they earned high wages in dead-end jobs and wanted something to spend them on. In this gap rock 'n' roll flourished' (*Revolt into Style*).

Tommy Steele's first recording *Rock with the Cavemen*, made in 1956, had limited success but his second, *Singing the Blues*, became top of the charts. Someone interviewed for *You'll Never be 16 Again* remembered;

You had to go to the record shop and queue for four Saturdays in a row to get your copy of *Singing the Blues*. I mean, he was the number one British person. If we went to family parties,

every cousin would get up and imitate Tommy Steele.

Colin MacInnes analyzed Steele's appeal to teenagers in *Encounter* (December 1957), calling him

The Pied Piper from Bermondsey . . . dressed in sky-blue jeans and a neon-hued shirting, who jumps, skips, doubles up and wriggles as he sings. At certain ritual gestures – a dig with the foot, a violent mopshake of the head – the teenagers massed from stalls to gallery utter a collective shriek of ectasy. Tommy has *sent* them: their idol has given bliss for gold.

MacInnes realized that pop music was the emblem of a new class.

Tommy Steele went on to become an all-round entertainer in the sixties, acting in pantomime, in films and with the Old Vic in *She Stoops to Conquer* in 1960. His greatest successes in later years were in musicals like *Half A Sixpence* in 1966, and in 1979 he was awarded an OBE for services to the theatre.

Ray Gosling

Teddy Boys first appeared in Britain in the early fifties, adopting rock 'n' roll as their music when it arrived from America. Youth was the main qualification. They were anti-authoritarian, generally working-class and they helped to increase the gulf between teenagers and adults. The phenomenon continued into the sixties, when new cults developed like the Mods and Rockers, Ton-up Boys and Hell's Angels, all distinguished by their different types of clothing, or 'gear'. Many of the young men owned more suits than their fathers.

Ray Gosling came from a working-class background in Northampton, growing up in a semi-detached house without an inside lavatory. 'Anything my parents couldn't afford they bought from the Co-op.' The family wash was done by boiling the clothes in a 'copper', mangling them and then drying them on a clothes horse in front of the fire. 'We had a radio, medium wave only, permanently tuned to the Home Service.' He and his friends met at the chip shop, which had

an old jukebox in the corner where we'd drop a twelve-sided threepenny bit and a record would plunk on a platter and play, very scratchily, 'I left my true love on blueberry hill . . .'. (*Personal Copy*.)

Gosling's life was changed as a teenager when he saw James Dean in the film *Rebel Without a Cause*, followed by *The Blackboard Jungle* in which Chuck Berry sang *Rock Around the Clock*. He remembers how

Rock 'n' roll sent me hell-bent to smash to smithereens everything my parents' generation had built.

Chuck Berry's song was 'like an electric shock . . .'. The teenagers in the cinema 'just stood in the aisles and howled'. Gosling was so shaken by the experiences that he wrote a letter to *The Times* saying that rock 'n roll was

more than music – it's a serious, outward and visible sign of a revolutionary change in the hearts of young people everywhere who are demanding the world be theirs. Rock 'n roll is smashing and it's going to smash all the fuddy-duddy civilization to smithereens. Rock 'n roll will change the world.'

He signed the letter 'a Teddy Boy'.

In Northampton, where Gosling lived, Teddy Boys dressed to outshine the Americans, who were still stationed in the area.

44 Ray Gosling.

We had to be flasher than them . . . my first shoes were dark navy-blue suede: brothel creepers they were called. . . My second pair of shoes were winkle-pickers – silver buckle and eight-inch-long pointed toes.

The old-fashioned barber who did a 'short back and sides' was no use to a Teddy Boy, who wanted styling. Hair was set in quiffs and

sideboards and curled with hot irons. 'We used to plaster it with coconut grease . . .'. Teds were clean shaven and always wore a white shirt, not a striped one. They often wore a silver chain round their necks and another round the wrist. They wore Edwardian styled

45 A Juke Box, like the one Ray Gosling and his friends patronised in the chip shop at Northampton.

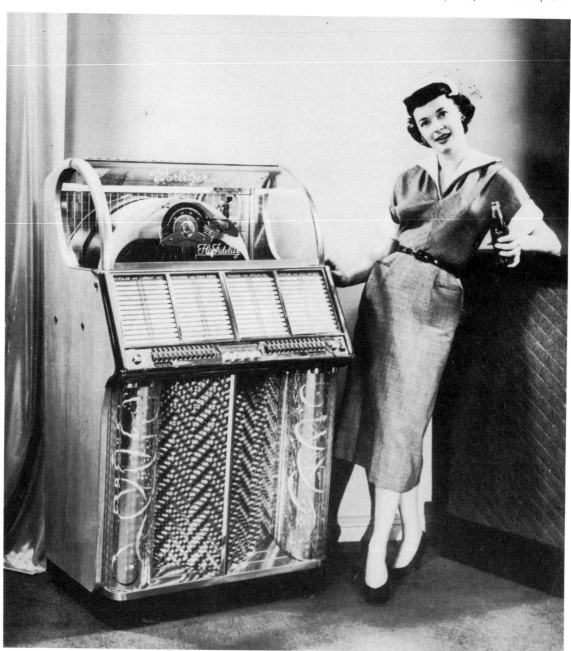

suits – Gosling had a blue jacket with a red lining, teamed with trousers which narrowed at the ankles bought at Montague Burton's. There were many variations in dress. From 1958 the 'Italian style' became popular and a new trend arrived from America, derived from Marlon Brando's film *The Wild One*, consisting of leather jackets, jeans, short hair cuts and moccasin shoes, 'in general appearance, in fact, like that of an urban, motorised cowboy' (Colin MacInnes, *Sharp Schmutter, The Twentieth Century*, August 1959).

Not all Teddy Boys were violent, but gangs of them often seemed threatening. There were many attempts to analyze the reasons for their appearance. Trevor Philpott, writing in *Picture Post*, thought that it was because many young people had monotonous jobs (1 April 1957). George Melly thought it might be because of

The lack of parental authority during the war? The breakdown of the working-class family as a strong social unit? . . . The effect of the bombing? Regret that the war was over too early to allow them to release their aggression under risk? (*Revolt into Style*).

In the sixties Ray Gosling had a varied career as manager of a pop group, factory worker, writer and community worker in Nottingham. Today he is a broadcaster and writer. Looking back he sees the fifties as a time when old loyalties were broken. The working class, who supported Eden's gunboat diplomacy at the time of Suez, became disillusioned when it failed and their loyalty to their country, right or wrong, was broken for ever.

YOU'VE NEVER HAD IT SO GOOD?

Between 1957 and 1963, when Harold Macmillan was Prime Minister, an 'affluent society' was born. New production techniques brought down the price of consumer goods and at the same time made higher wages possible. Between 1955 and 1960 basic weekly wage rates rose 25 per cent, but if overtime was taken into account the rise was 34 per cent. Prices rose only by about 15 per cent. Some goods, like cars, television sets, refrigerators and washing machines actually came down in price.

Social habits changed with the new prosperity. Cheaper household appliances and the discovery of detergents and synthetic fabrics saved women from long hours doing washing. The number of households with refrigerators rose from eight per cent in 1956 to 33 per cent in 1962. The sales of frozen food doubled at the end of the fifties. People now bought frozen peas, chips, fish fingers and ice-cream instead of tinned salmon, tinned peaches and baked beans. Homes were better designed and equipped, and generally more comfortable. Central heating or stoves burning smokeless fuel replaced open coal fires. Flats were popular for council or private purchase and were often given no fireplaces. By the mid-fifties 15 new towns were being built.

After the war only a small proportion of the population had been entitled to one week's paid leave a year, in addition to Bank Holidays. By the end of the fifties almost everyone received two weeks. Saturday morning work was also being phased out. Over half the population went away on holiday each year, many of them to the Continent, as prices were coming down and the foreign currency allowance was doubled to £100 per person in 1955. Linked with foreign travel was

an increasing interest in foreign food – British tastes had previously been very conservative. Harry Hopkins reports seeing in a café window 'Try Pizza and Chips – the Italian Welsh Rarebit' (*The New Look*). Expresso Bars were themselves Italian in origin. As import restrictions slackened, foreign goods became available again in Britain.

46 More people were able to take holidays abroad in the late fifties.

Television sets were a rarity in 1950 but 75 per cent of the population had them by 1961. Commercial television influenced the nation's spending habits and the medium had an adverse effect on some other forms of entertainment. Looking back in 1988, John Wain believed that television was anti-literary.

Not all Brendan Behan's inborn flair for dramatic writing would have brought him the fame that he gained in five minutes by appearing on *Panorama* when drunk (*Sunday Times* 6 March 1988).

Television was also ultimately responsible for the decline in the popularity of the cinema and the demise of illustrated weeklys like *Picture Post*. Between 1954 and 1959 over 800 cinemas closed and News Theatres disappeared for good. Ex-*Picture Post* writers and photographers like Dan Farson and Trevor Philpott joined television instead. The old commercial lending libraries were another casualty. Books became more pictorial, leading to the 'coffee table' books of the sixties and the Sunday colour supplements.

Harold Macmillan, who was Conservative Prime Minister from 1957 to 1963, was given the credit for the affluent society and the phrase attributed to him, 'You've never had it so good', was used as a symbol of his Ministry by the press. Mary Quant was one of the new young people who made their mark in the fifties. Many more were to join her in the sixties.

47 The Queen opens Subscriber Trunk Dialling in Britain at Bristol in 1958. The service was extended to London by 1961 and gradually to the rest of the country.

Harold Macmillan (1894-1986)

Harold Macmillan was a fascinating personality, publicly self-confident but privately introspective, a strange mixture of the hard-headed professional politician and the amateurish, country gentleman sort of public servant. . . . He mesmerised the public with his lugubrious wit and epigrammatic phrase and by 1959 his political ascendancy seemed all but complete. (Alan Sked and Chris Cook, *Post-War Britain*.)

48 Harold Macmillan, Chancellor of the Exchequer, holds up one of the new Premium Savings Bonds, November 1956.

Macmillan came from a publishing family and first became an MP in 1924. He served in the Conservative government during the early fifties as Minister of Housing and Local Government in 1951, Minister of Defence in 1954 and Foreign Secretary in 1955. As Chancellor of the Exchequer between 1955 and 1957 he was responsible for introducing Premium Bonds (1957). He was in a position to observe the strained relationship between Churchill and Eden in the early fifties, writing in his diary, 'It's particularly tiresome to be forced to act as a sort of mediator between Churchill and Eden' (5 October 1954).

Macmillan survived the *débâcle* of Suez in 1956. Although he had supported Eden's use of force, he changed his policy almost overnight, realizing that 'a profound miscalculation of the likely reaction in Washington' had been made. He became Prime Minister in 1957 after Eden's illness and resignation. Macmillan took over at a difficult time but he was determined to revive the fortunes of the Party. His first task was to patch up Britain's relationship with America, but in no way did he apologize for Suez. He said to Eisenhower,

You need us for ourselves, for the Commonwealth, and as leaders of Europe. But chiefly because without a common front and true partnership between us I doubt whether the principles we believe in can win (Quoted in *Post-War Britain*).

Macmillan quickly established control over his cabinet and remained as Prime Minister for over six years, restoring the country's self-confidence after Suez. He earned himself the nickname 'SuperMac' and was a good speaker. He was the first Prime Minister to master the art of the television interview. John Colville writes,

Macmillan was a superb performer in an age which could boast of Olivier, Gielgud and Alec Guinness. He was scarcely their inferior in the art, but he was not an actor in the sense that he played a part in which he disbelieved. On the contrary he chose the role and he performed it with style and professional polish (*The New Elizabethan.*)

The newscaster Alastair Burnet remembers Macmillan's first appearances on television, when he pretended to be 'just a sleepy-eyed old bookseller, baffled by the hyper-sophisticated world of television'. (*Coming to You Live*).

It was Macmillan's decision that Britain should have an independent deterrent and a British hydrogen bomb was successfully tested in 1957. The 1957 White Paper on Defence promised to end National Service by 1960 and reduce the size of the army. Macmillan said to the House that, although there had been some advantages to National Service,

it also has great weaknesses and great wastefulness. There are too many people under this system learning and then leaving when they have learned . . . (*Hansard*, 17 April 1957).

He described the hydrogen bomb in a Party

49 Zephyr and Zodiac cars on the production line of Ford's, Dagenham. Car ownership increased in the late fifties and the first stretch of the M1 was opened in 1959.

Political Broadcast as 'our best guarantee of safety from attack and so really the best guarantee of peace' (4 January 1958). The defence budget could now be reduced and Britain would no longer need to rely on America for protection. The Liberals were the only party to oppose the deterrent and the Campaign for Nuclear Disarmament was formed to convince the Labour Party, in particular, to oppose the policy.

The failure of Suez changed Macmillan's political thinking with regard to the Commonwealth. By the end of the fifties Ghana, Malaysia, Singapore, and Cyprus had gained independence and Macmillan made the speech saying 'a wind of change is blowing through Africa' in February 1960. The Macmillan government was successful in persuading the newly independent countries to join the Commonwealth.

Commonwealth affairs led Macmillan to disregard what was happening in Europe and the European Economic Community went ahead without Britain. However, he improved diplomatic relations with the Soviet Union. In November 1958 the Soviet leader Kruschev gave the Allies six months months to withdraw their troops from Berlin, a confrontation which made war a possibility. Macmillan visited Moscow in 1959, so becoming the first Western Head of State to go there in peace time. Although nothing tangible was achieved then or at the Geneva Conference which followed, Kruschev did not pursue the ultimatum and Macmillan gained publicity as a peacemaker.

At the next election in 1959 Conservative policy was based on Britain's new prosperity and their hopes to double the standard of living of the people within a generation. Election posters read 'Life is better with the Conservatives. . . Don't let Labour ruin it.' The Conservatives gained a decisive victory in the election, with a majority of 100 seats. It was a personal triumph for Macmillan.

The Conservative election promises, however, were not fulfilled. Macmillan's second Ministry failed to deal effectively with inflation and the country was rebuffed by the French when attempting to join the Common Market in 1963. Macmillan's last months in office were marred by illness and the Profumo scandal. Labour returned to power in 1964, ending 13 years of Conservative rule.

Mary Quant (1934-   )

Fashion designer Mary Quant was one of the personalities who created the image of 'Swinging London' which became current in the late fifties and early sixties. Up to 1955, when she and Alexander Plunkett-Greene opened their shop 'Bazaar' in King's Road, Chelsea, women's fashions had been formal and expensive, dictated by designers like Dior and Balenciaga in Paris or Hardy Amies in London. Make-up made girls look as old as their mothers. Hats and gloves were essential for a visit to town. Hair was 'set' regularly. Philippa Pullar remembers how she could 'never go out in the wind or rain in case the curls came out' (Golden Butterflies). Underwear was nearly as constricting as it had been in Victorian times.

Quant was one of the first designers to cater for the young, who now had more money to spend and were delighted to find someone designing lively, colourful clothes. Her shop was an immediate success. She realized that mass-produced clothes need not be dull and created a new image – a complete head-to-toe style, incorporating cheap materials like plastic for boots and handbags, which the

50 Mary Quant (seated right) and her husband Alexander Plunkett-Greene (standing right) at the latter's restaurant in 1956.

young could afford to buy.

Mary Quant had met Alexander Plunket Greene at Goldsmiths' College, when they were both students. After leaving college she found work with a milliner where she was paid £2 10s a week.

There was never any money for food and I spent nothing on clothes. I made all these myself, sitting up most of the night to remake the same dresses year after year and try to give them something of a new look (*Quant by Quant*).

Quant and Plunkett-Greene soon had many friends in Chelsea, among them Archie McNair, who invited Alexander to be his partner in a new coffee bar in King's Road. The bar soon became a centre of social life in Chelsea and the two men decided to open a boutique with Mary. They were able to buy premises in King's Road for £8000.

Jacqmar
10 GROSVENOR ST · LONDON W.1 · Mayfair 6111

DALLAS, by Monte Sano – New York's celebrated
designer, who contributes this suave coat
to Jacqmar's International Collection,
proving conclusively that a fitted coat is feminine
and flattering. In white, Siamese blue,
watermelon pink and acid yellow tweed, all finely
etched with black. Versatile collar, brigand cuffs,
and indented waist, tucked and clasped with
narrow calf belt. Ready-to-wear at 34 gns.

HAT BY SASK THARRUP.

51 Fashion was formal in the days before Mary Quant's boutique – a Jacqumar advertisement, 1955.

Mary Quant did not like the fashions of the day.

To me adult appearance was very unattractive. . . . It was something I knew I didn't want to grow into. . . I wanted everyone to retain the grace of a child, so I created clothes that allowed people to run, to jump, to leap, to retain this precious freedom. (Quoted in *The Fifties* by Peter Lewis.)

When 'Bazaar' opened it was an immediate success, partly because the owners had not priced the stock correctly and were underselling every other shop in London. Mary had only designed one item for the

opening – a pair of house-pyjamas, but these were immediately photographed by *Harper's Bazaar*.

The difficulties of keeping the shop stocked with the right kind of merchandise led Mary to design garments herself.

I also started going to a few frantic evening classes on cutting. I bought the materials at Harrods as no one had told me about buying cloth wholesale.

She had to sell the garments before she could afford to buy any more material. Her bedsitting room was her workroom and her two cats used to eat the paper patterns.

It took me some time to discover that the tissue paper used to make these patterns is manufactured from some by-product of fish bones!

'Bazaar' stayed open late.

. . . people loved it. They loved coming up to the shop with husbands and boy friends late at night after a good dinner and looking through our things. . .

As Mary wanted the shop window to look different, she had special figures made to display the clothes. Alexander's restaurant, which had opened at the same time as 'Bazaar', also did well. Prince Rainier and Grace Kelly had a rendevouz there before they were married, and on another occasion Brigitte Bardot came with Jacques Charrier. King's Road became the meeting place of the 'Chelsea Set', who became the trend-setters for the next decade.

By the early sixties 'Swinging London' was known throughout the world. For Mary Quant and Alexander Plunkett-Greene, who by this time had sold his restaurant, it brought great success and the 'Bazaar' look was copied internationally. Mary writes in her auto-biography,

The clothes I made happened to fit in exactly with the teenage trend, with pop records and

52 People began to go regularly to the hairdresser in the late fifties. A photograph of Raymond – Mr Teezie-Weezie – at work.

expresso bars and jazz clubs. . . Never before have the young set the pace as they do now. Snobbery has gone out of fashion, and in our shops you will find duchesses jostling with typists to buy the same dresses.

Boutiques were a reaction against department stores and expensive fashions. Within a year or two of 'Bazaar' opening, John Stephen opened his first shop in Carnaby Street and small boutiques opened everywhere, providing original fashions that everyone could afford. Fashion became classless and shopping habits were revolutionized.

PRELUDE TO THE SIXTIES

The liberating effect of full employment and prosperity, coupled with the growing influence of the young, led to a rebellion against authority during the fifties. In the sixties the rebellion became explicit and political. Prosperity created a new elite class of successful young people in new professions – boutique owners, photographers, hair-

53 *Picture Post* during the fifties. When the magazine folded in 1957, Sir Edward Hulton said that commercial television had taken away many of its readers.

dressers, restaurant owners and those in the entertainment industry. The fifties also saw the start of the democratization of the monarchy. As the Queen and Royal Family became more accessible, so some of the mystique of the monarchy was lost, a process which was to continue until the present day.

A liberalization of outlook was also taking place. Lord Wolfenden's report recommending a more liberal attitude to homosexuality was completed in 1957, but not acted on for some years. 1957 also saw the introduction of a Bill to end hanging, which did not become law until 1965. One of the first signs of the relaxation of the Victorian moral code was that the publishers of *Lady Chatterley's Lover* were cleared of an obscenity charge in 1959, leading the way to the abolition of film and theatre censorship in the sixties.

Thirteen years of Conservative rule from 1951 to 1964 brought new prosperity, but many who had been in the Services during the war and voted Labour afterwards had hoped for a new, egalitarian world. They were disappointed instead to find a 'stampede for wealth, great opportunities for ambition, a return to inequality', in the Macmillan era (Neal Ascherson, *The Observer* 1987). In 1950 the dismemberment of Empire had begun, although Britain still had a role as a world power. Disillusionment with politicians increased after Suez and pressure groups such as CND sprang up – a trend which would accelerate in the sixties.

54 Nostalgia for the fifties – People in fifties clothes pose round a car of the period during the Victoria and Albert Museum's Festival of the 1950s in 1988.

The economic promise of Macmillan's premiership turned out to be illusory. It was too good to last and by his second term defects in the economy were apparent. Britain's share of world trade declined and prices rose ten per cent compared with Germany's two per cent. British exports rose by only 28 per cent, compared with those of Germany (150 per cent) and Italy (180 per cent). Productivity was down compared with that of Germany, Italy and Japan. It had also been a bad mistake to ignore the European Economic Community when favourable terms of entry were available. General de Gaulle rejected the British application for membership in 1963.

The fifties were a gateway to the sixties. Many of the changes in society for which the sixties are known had their roots in the earlier decade. The British began to question themselves and the nature of their society in a way not seen before in the twentieth century.

DATE LIST

1950 North Korea invades South Korea.
1951 Conservatives replace Labour at election. Churchill Prime Minister.
Festival of Britain.
Defection of Burgess and Maclean.
Last Britains leave Abadan Oil Refinery.
1952 Death of George VI and accession of Elizabeth II.
US Hydrogen bomb test.
1953 Death of Stalin.
Coronation of Queen Elizabeth.
Everest climbed by Hillary and Tensing.
1954 Nasser gains power in Egypt.
Roger Bannister beats the four-minute mile.
Publication of *Lucky Jim*.
1955 Emergency in Cyprus.
Eden becomes Prime Minister.
'Bazaar' opens.
Commercial television starts.

1956 Suez Crisis.
Hungarian Revolution.
First performance of *Look Back in Anger*.
Tommy Steele discovered.
1957 Macmillan becomes Prime Minister on Eden's resignation.
Testing of British hydrogen bomb.
First Aldermaston March.
Premium Bonds start.
Wolfenden Report.
Publication of *Room at the Top* by John Braine.
1958 Race riots in Nottingham and Notting Hill Gate.
Fuchs crosses Antartica.
1959 Conservatives increase their majority at election.
Singapore becomes self governing.
Castro seizes power in Cuba.

Book List

Allsop, Kenneth, *The Angry Decade* (Peter Owen, 1958)

Amis, Kingsley, *Lucky Jim* (Victor Gollancz, 1954)

Banham, Mary (ed.) and Hillier, Bevis, *A Tonic to the Nation* (Thames & Hudson, 1976)

Beaton, Cecil, *The Strenuous Years* (Weidenfeld & Nicolson, 1973)

Beaton, Cecil, *The Restless Years* (Weidenfeld & Nicolson, 1976)

Boyle, Andrew, *The Climate of Treason* (Hutchinson, 1979)

Bradbury, Malcolm, *Eating People is Wrong* (Secker & Warburg, 1959)

Braine, John, *Room at the Top* (Eyre & Spottiswood, 1957)

Braithwaite, E.R., *To Sir, With Love* (Bodley Head, 1959)

Braithwaite, E.R., *Reluctant Neighbours* (Bodley Head, 1972)

Colville, John, *The New Elizabethans* (Collins, 1977)

Dimbleby, Jonathan, *Richard Dimbleby* (Hodder & Stoughton, 1975)

Everett, Peter, *You'll Never be Sixteen Again* (BBC, 1986)

Gosling, Ray, *Personal Copy* (Faber, 1980)

Hopkins, Harry, *The New Look* (Secker & Warburg, 1964)

James, Robert R., *Anthony Eden* (Weidenfeld & Nicolson, 1986)

Knightley, Philip, *The Second Oldest Profession* (André Deutsch, 1986)

Lewis, Peter, *The Fifties* (Heinemann, 1987)

MacInnes, Colin, *Absolute Beginners* (MacGibbon & Kee, 1959)

MacInnes, Colin, *City of Spades* (MacGibbon & Kee, 1957)

Macmillan, Harold, *Tides of Fortune* (Macmillan, 1969)

McMillan, James, *The Way it Changed* (William Kimber, 1987)

Marwick, Arthur, *British Society Since 1945* (Penguin, 1982)

Melly, George, *Owning Up* (Weidenfeld & Nicolson, 1965)

Melly, George, *Revolt into Style* (Allen Lane, 1970)

Montgomery, John, *The Fifties* (George Allen & Unwin, 1965).

Norden, Denis, *Coming to you Live* (Methuen, 1985)

Osborne, John, *A Better Class of Person* (Faber & Faber, 1981)

Osborne, John, *Look Back in Anger* (Faber & Faber, 1957)

Quant, Mary, *Quant by Quant* (Cassell, 1966)

Royle, Trevor, *The Best Years of Their Lives* (Michael Joseph, 1986)

Russell Taylor, John, *Anger and After* (Penguin, 1963)

Sked, Alan and Cook, Chris, *Post War Britain: A Political History*, (Penguin, 1979)

Thomas, Leslie, *In My Wildest Dreams* (Penguin, 1986)

Vickers, Hugo, *Cecil Beaton* (Weidenfeld & Nicolson, 1985)

INDEX

Figures in italic refer to illustration numbers